Discover stories of fortunate events and happy coincidences in this unique collection of coloring pages from illustrator R.J. Hampson.

This book contains 25 original hand-drawn illustrations for you to color. For artists, coloring enthusiasts, and those looking for a little unexpected joy!

See more at rjhampson.com

russelljamesart

Published by Hop Skip Jump. PO Box 1324 Buderim Queensland Australia 4556
First published 2023. Copyright © 2023 R.J. Hampson.

All Rights Reserved. Without limiting the rights under copyright reserved above, no part of this publication may be reproduced, stored in or introduced into a retrieval system, or transmitted, in any form or by any means (electronic, mechanical, photocopying, recording or otherwise), without the prior written permission of both the copyright owner and the above publisher of this book. The only exception is by a reviewer who may share short excerpts in a review.

ISBN: 978-1-922472-31-1

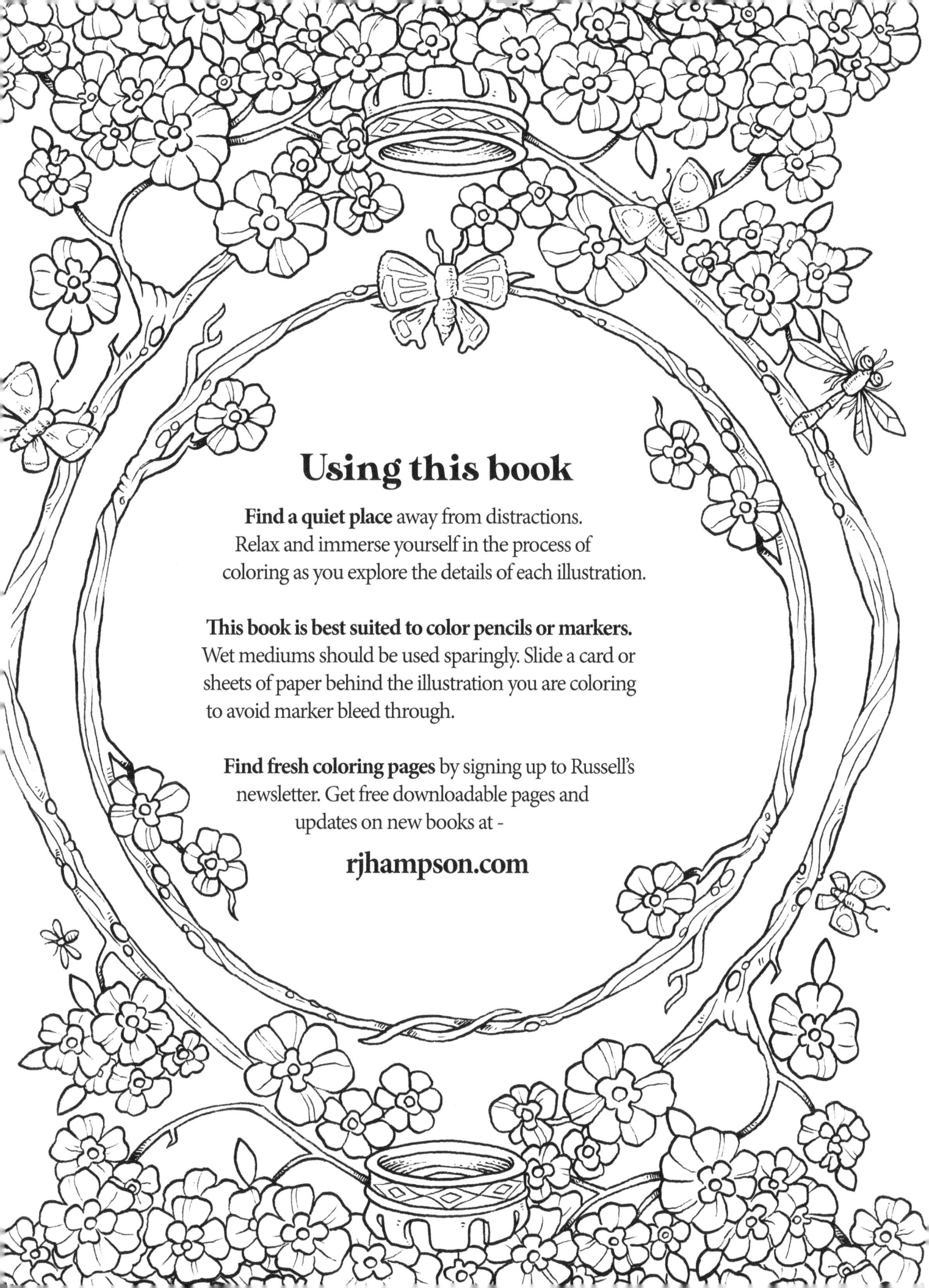

Using this book

Find a quiet place away from distractions. Relax and immerse yourself in the process of coloring as you explore the details of each illustration.

This book is best suited to color pencils or markers. Wet mediums should be used sparingly. Slide a card or sheets of paper behind the illustration you are coloring to avoid marker bleed through.

Find fresh coloring pages by signing up to Russell's newsletter. Get free downloadable pages and updates on new books at -

rjhampson.com

MOVING HOUSE

EUREKA

OPEN SESAME

WINTER BLOSSOMS

WINTER JOY

SWEET AS HONEY

THE SUNSHINE IS A GLORIOUS BIRTH

PERFECT TIMING

THE QUEST

JUST IN TIME FOR TEA

JUST IN TIME FOR TEA

THE ALCHEMIST

WILD IS THE MUSIC

A VITAL CLUE

NIGHT LIGHTS

A ROOM WITH A VIEW

SHANGRI-LA

CANDY CANE LANE

CHINCHILLA CHA-CHA

LOTUS DREAMING

CHRISTMAS GIFTS

LOVE THY NEIGHBOUR

ONE PERFECT DAY

SUDDENLY

FREEDOM ON A STRING

Relax, chill out, and unwind!

Find new coloring pages by signing up to R.J. Hampson's newsletter.
Get free downloadable pages, monthly coloring sheets,
and updates on new books at -

rjhampson.com/coloring

Thanks for choosing this coloring book.
If you enjoyed it, please consider leaving a review.
It will help to let more people in on the experience
plus you'd certainly make this illustrator very happy!

More books in this series

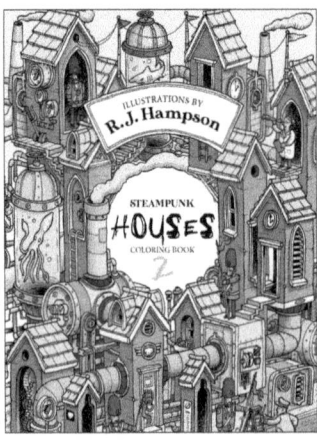

COLLECT THEM ALL!

See flip-throughs for all coloring books at **rjhampson.com**

www.ingramcontent.com/pod-product-compliance
Lightning Source LLC
Chambersburg PA
CBHW041221240426
43661CB00012B/1108